Manufactured in Mexico
February 2012

ISBN 978-1-935703-59-4

10 9 8 7 6 5 4 3 2 1

www.getoutthebook.com

GET OUT!

I'm Trying to F**k Your Mother

A TRAGI-COMEDY

BY JON STONE

ILLUSTRATED BY MICHEL ROSEAU

The kids are all sleeping.

Let's go to bed early.

What peeks through the door?

A head that is curly.

March back to your bed—
let's end this charade.
You're cute as a button,
but Dad's getting laid.

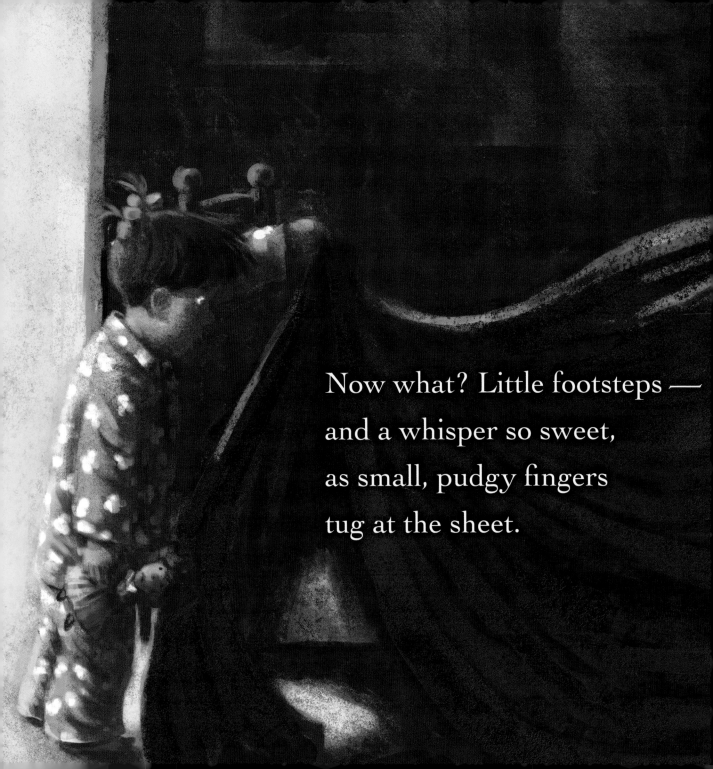

Now what? Little footsteps —
and a whisper so sweet,
as small, pudgy fingers
tug at the sheet.

I'll stay under here
until we both smother.
I'm not coming out
'til I fuck your mother.

We played the same game
to make you—in this bed!
Right now I'm wishing
I had a blow job instead.

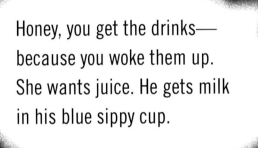

Honey, you get the drinks—
because you woke them up.
She wants juice. He gets milk
in his blue sippy cup.

Sorry Mom woke you,
she's a bit of a moaner.
I'd run to the kitchen,
but you'd see Daddy's boner.

There's nothing to fear.
Close your eyes and rest.
(Though you might see a ghost
before I see Mommy's breasts.)

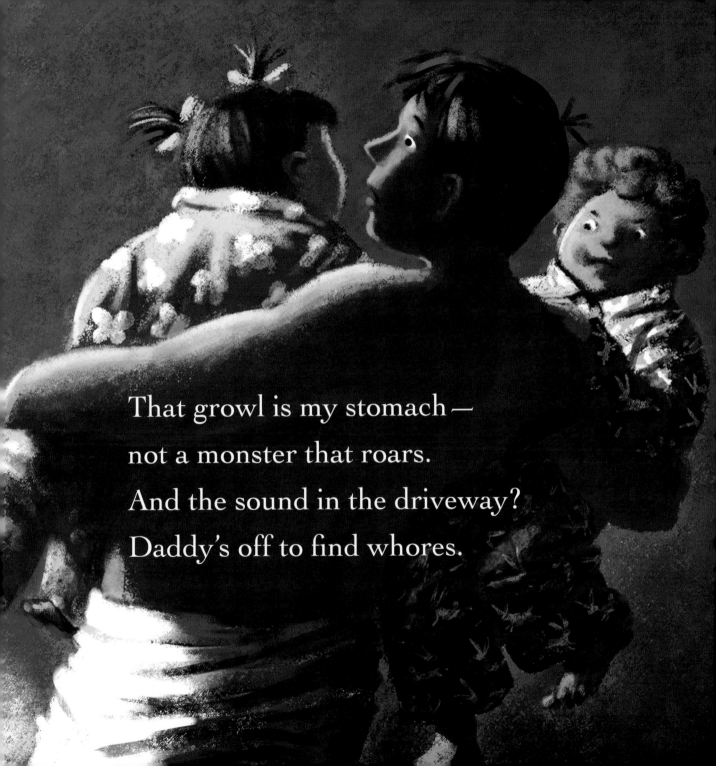

That growl is my stomach —
not a monster that roars.
And the sound in the driveway?
Daddy's off to find whores.

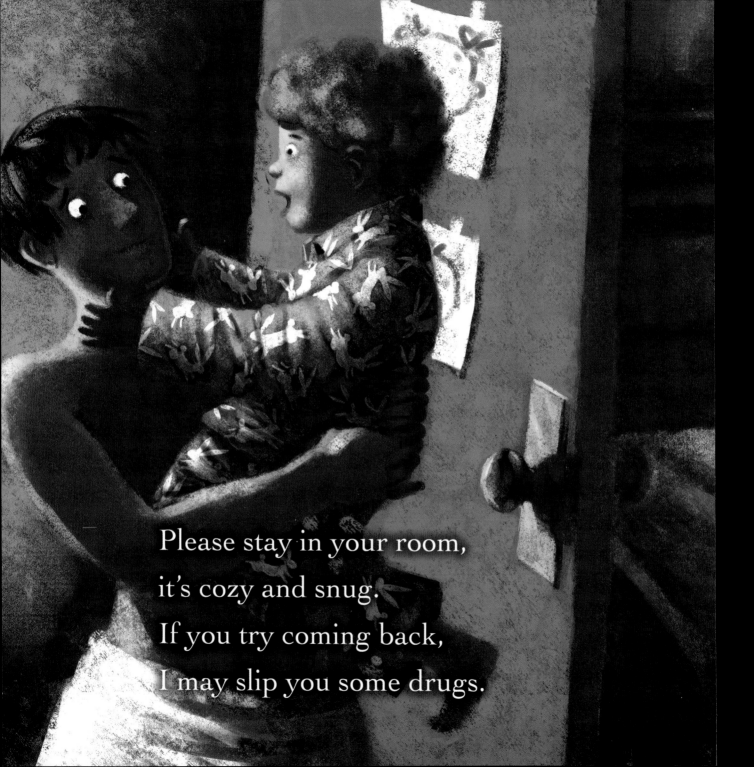

Please stay in your room,
it's cozy and snug.
If you try coming back,
I may slip you some drugs.

Of course Daddy loves you,
and I'm thrilled you were born.
It's just that I miss
getting off without porn.

PLEEEASE?

Harold and his crayon
that makes things real?
I've got something purple
for Mommy to feel.

The Little Engine that Could?
I totally relate.
I *know* that I can
with just 10 minutes straight.

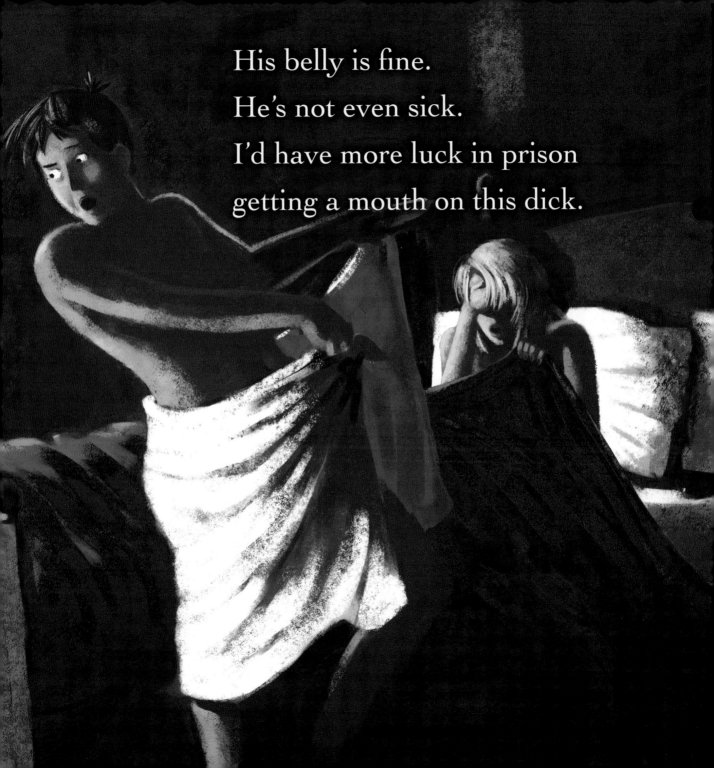

His belly is fine.

He's not even sick.

I'd have more luck in prison

getting a mouth on this dick.

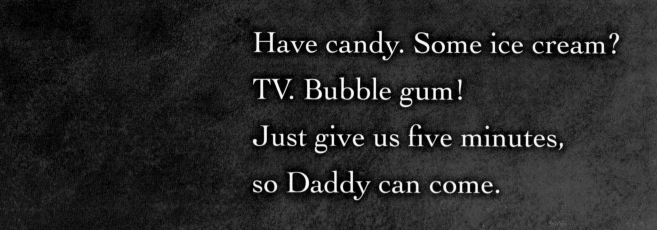

Have candy. Some ice cream?
TV. Bubble gum!
Just give us five minutes,
so Daddy can come.

Want a bite...?

That was SO NOT five minutes
'til you pounded and screamed.
You may be in our bed,
but Mom's still getting reamed.

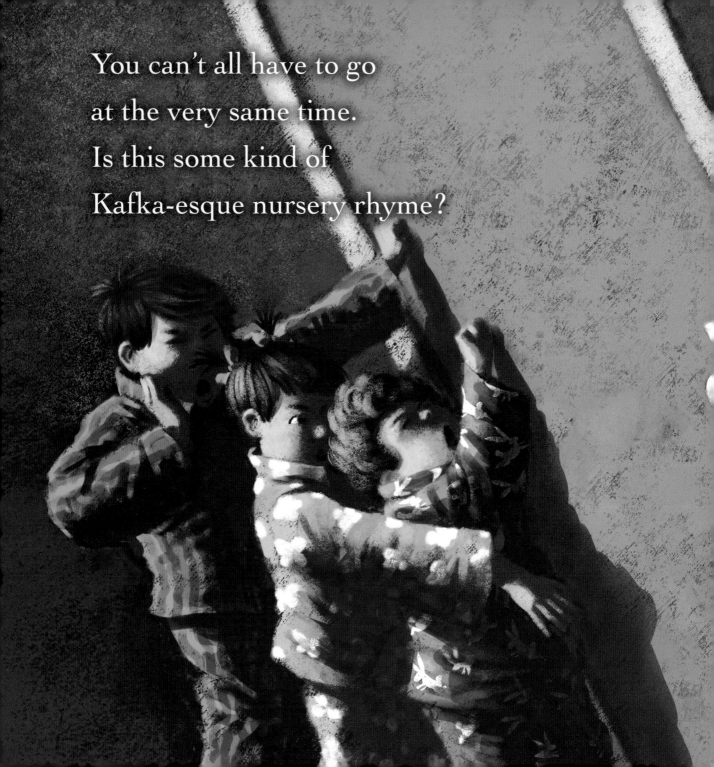

You can't all have to go
at the very same time.
Is this some kind of
Kafka-esque nursery rhyme?

You took over our bed,
now we're stuck on the tile
You had drinks, you had treats.
I'll have mine doggy style.

Babe, Daddy loves you…
And your sister. And brother!
But GO AWAY PLEASE.
I'm trying to fuck your mother.

We're finally alone!

I'm so happy I could weep…

Lotion

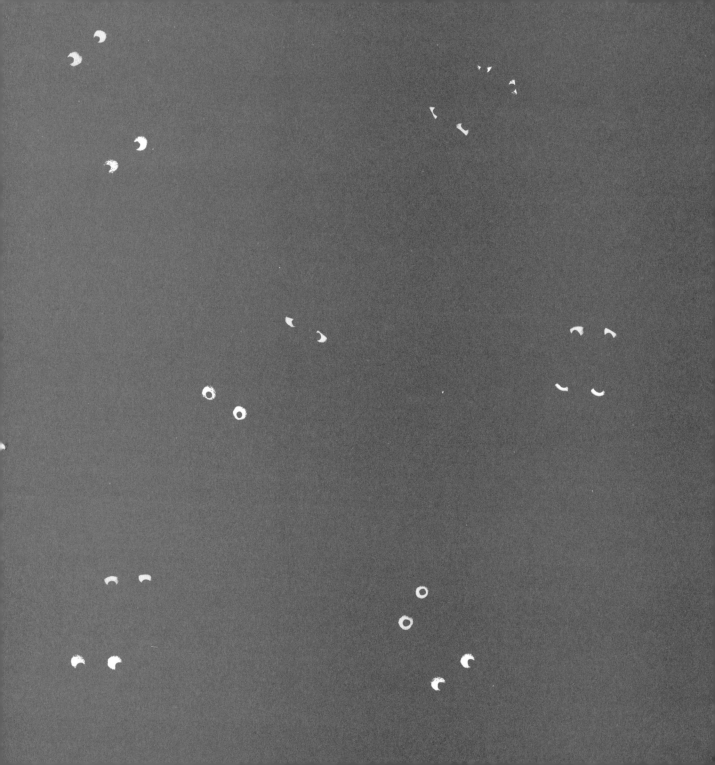